A

GEOGRAPHY

of

SOULS

LIST OF SOURCES OF QUOTATIONS

Elizabeth Bishop, "The Riverman," *Complete Poems* (London: Chatto & Windus, 1983; rpt. 1991): 107.

Kate Atkinson, *Human Croquet* (London: Black Swan Books, a division of Transworld Publishers, 1998): 13. All rights reserved.

Sherman Alexie, "A Good Story," *The Lone Ranger and Tonto Fistfight in Heaven* (New York: Harper Perennial, 1994): 143. It is here reprinted by arrangement with The Atlantic Monthly Press.

Freidrich Nietzsche, *The Gay Science: With a Prelude in German Rhymes and an Appendix of Songs* (1887) ed. Bernard Williams (Cambridge: Cambridge UP, 2001): 119

Henry Rollins, *See A Grown Man Cry Now Watch Him Die* (Los Angeles: 2.13.61 Publications, 1997): 165.

Mark Lanegan, "House a Home," track 3 on *Whiskey for the Holy Ghost* (Sub Pop, 1993. SPCD78/249).

The Koran, As-Sajda (Sura 32, verse 11).

Virginia Woolf, *Orlando* (1928; Harmondsworth: Penguin, 1993): 89.

David Treuer, *Little* (London: Granta, 1995): 183.

Sam Shepard, "You I Have No Distance From," *Cruising Paradise* (London: Secker & Warburg, 1996): 65-66.

Emily Dickinson, "There's a certain Slant of light," *Complete Poems* (London: Faber, 1975): 118.

Paul Durcan, "Sunday's Well," *Sam's Cross* (Portmarnock: Profile Poetry, 1978): 21. Rpt. in *The Selected Paul Durcan*, ed. Edna Longley (Belfast: Blackstaff Press, 1982): 71.

Nick Cave, "The Secret Life of the Love Song," on *The Secret Life of the Love Song* and *The Word Made Flesh: Two Lectures by Nick Cave* (King Mob, 1999. KMOB7). Published in Nick Cave, *The Complete Lyrics 1978-2001* (London: Penguin, 2001): 7.

Gregor von Rezzori, *Memoirs of an Anti-Semite: A Novel in Five Stories* (1969; London: Picador, 1983): 1.

A

GEOGRAPHY

of

SOULS

KATHLEEN McCRACKEN

THISTLEDOWN PRESS

Canadian Cataloguing in Publication Data

McCracken, Kathleen, 1962 –
A geography of souls

Poems.
ISBN 1-894345-39-8
I. Title.
PS8575.C73G46 2002   C811'.54   C2001-911596-2
PR9199.3.M295G46 2002

Cover photograph: *Man on Horse on Beach at Irish Moss Harvest,
near Cavendish Prince Edward Island, Canada*
© Mark Tomalty/Masterfile

Typeset by Thistledown Press Ltd.
Printed and bound in Canada by AGMV Marquis

Thistledown Press Ltd.
633 Main Street
Saskatoon, Saskatchewan
S7H 0J8

Thistledown Press gratefully acknowledges the financial assistance of the Canada Council for the Arts, the Saskatchewan Arts Board, and the Government of Canada through the Book Publishing Industry Development Program for its publishing program.

ACKNOWLEDGEMENTS

Acknowledgements are due to the editors of the following publications in which versions of some of these poems first appeared: *Writing Ulster, New Orleans Review, Honest Ulsterman, Poetry Ireland, Fortnight, Grain* and *The Malahat Review*. "A Tree Asleep At The Centre Of A Field" received honourable mention in the Canadian National Poetry Contest and is published in *Vintage 97/98* (1998). "Green Pool With Lightning" was published in *The White Page/An Bhileog Bhan: Twentieth-Century Irish Women Poets* (1999) and "Good Friday, Belfast, 1998" in *You Can't Eat Flags For Breakfast* (2001).

I would like to thank Bernard and Mary Loughlin at the Tyrone Guthrie Centre, Co. Monaghan, for their hospitality while this collection got under way. For advice and support of various kinds, I also wish to thank Paul Farrelly, Paul Durcan, Stephen Milligen, Robert and Shirley McCracken, Chris McCracken, Marie McCracken, Joseph McMinn, Ronnie Bailie and Arthur Aughey.

To Seán Virgo, whose editorial skill and generosity of spirit are unrivalled, my deepest gratitude.

CONTENTS

PART ONE

PART TWO

I need a virgin mirror
no one's ever looked at,
that's never looked back at anyone,
to flash up the spirits' eyes
and help me recognize them.

— Elizabeth Bishop, *The Riverman*

And what about the wolves? What happened to them? (Just
because you can't see something doesn't mean it isn't there.)

— Kate Atkinson, *Human Croquet*

Part One

We are all given something to compensate for what we have lost.
— Sherman Alexie
The Lone Ranger And Tonto Fistfight In Heaven

SAUDADE

If I could come home to you now I would.
The red and white and blue sails
of fishing boats out from Algarve
the pots and nets and cracker-jack days
breaking open in the laps of Spanish widows.

If I could come home to you
Lisbon, Leipzig, Belize, Barcelona
all night I would tell you stories
of the red Mojave, the blue Cascades
the white diadem of Canada's antlered head.

The head, the heart, the hands —
what I would say to you, over and over in the dark
is that every hairpin turn brings you back to where you started
homesick for somewhere you've never been
for everything you can't put a name to.

Mouth full of hunger and sluicing with the arguments
itinerants trade in their jungles of trestles and night fires
I take my head in my hands and cut out of the dark
that heart-shaped country emblazoned
on the sleeve of every Polish-Portuguese-Venezuelan-Thai
North American from Micmac to Spokane

the motley each of us wears
sailing home to you, now, if we could.

Annaghmakerrig, 1991

10

EXILE WOMAN

In the absence
of that other country
she has learned to live
in this one —
Knockagh of the monuments and murders,
Wolf Hill teeming
with the ghosts
of *canis lupus*,
the urban eclipses
of Black Mountain.

Without sumach and maple
she has planted magnolia, laburnum
eucalyptus, drenched throats open
to the sea. In place of fresh
water and limestone there is
salt, basalt, and the octagonal shapes
of two island outposts
at war with themselves.

When she tends to Antrim's
walled garden
a continent turns over
inside her. Its name
is the name of the only man
it is not possible to leave.

Great nephew, first husband
he will draw and quarter
plant and harvest

the kind of exile woman
I am telling you about
the minute she sets down
at Gander, Newfoundland,
coat already seeded
with corn and tobacco.

SKUSHNO

Rezzori scouting the Russian steppe
for signs of the winter wolf, his turncoat colours
a flashy dissolve into white on white

could be Carson scouting Craigantlet's snowy sawback
for a gap to let the sight-lines run
clear down to Dundalk

or Crowfoot looking west-north-west from Calgary
across the frozen great divide then setting
his face hard against plains.

There's none of us surprised by the boredom or bewilderment.
It's like driving home over and again
vision narrowed to the floating white line
with only the light different and the odometer clocking
the space between this and the time before.

Cold wind in a dust mote skull. *Skushno.*
Steps up to the front door swept clean
and behind, everything on the periphery
(everything you've missed before):
bayonets in the tumbleweed, lightning under stone.

"Do you know a tree's roots
are approximately equivalent
to the span of its branches?

That the Tower of Babel was a ziggurat
observatory, prison, asylum,
lighthouse in an ocean of prairie?

That a cubit measures less than an arm's length,
is four or five or six palm breadths
depending on the lay of your hand?"

Suppose I did but somewhere had forgotten —
like remembering the once-off, indelible detail
differently every time

or hearing your own voice
rehearsed in the angular inflections
of hard men in from Skye.

The mind is a Chinese box, a spate of sand
inscribed with hieroglyphs, a thorn, a madder-tipped
torpedo, a flight of moving stairs

we walk down backwards to be
out there in the dark and speaking
in tongues, making answers like

"What's torn down is easy built back up
almost the same again," or "That pine's a cracker
3D reproduction of the way I know you think it ought to be."

Or so they'd have us believe,
our sign painters, our holy men.
What's freely chosen is yours to live with
so you'd better make the right
choice and stick with it.

It's a straight road all the way, no
switchbacks, turnpikes, cutoffs.
Just keep your eye on that clean white line
— gleam of tigers' eyes and immanence —
and you're home free.

So they'd have us believe,
our clear-sighted compañeros
who don't need to see the sun
going down on the left, the moon
coming up on the right.

Or like the madman in the marketplace
his lantern burning
— *I am looking for God, I am looking for God* —
feel in the bones the brief history that is time
turn like a tide against itself.

Faith without evidence, the inscrutable
certitude of the converted and the damned.
Say it one way or say it another
it all comes down

to that afternoon in the Austrian Alps,
siphoning the thin air of mountain climbs

til you're over the top and back again. Full stop.
Eternity now. Then catching sight of your alter
ego in the window of a tavern
in a town you're no longer sure
you can call your own.

TALKING TO THE MILKMAN

The answer to your question is:
it might be Irish and it might be Onondaga,
the language we speak in dreams, without hesitation.

ALCATRAZ

Tell me, Kola, haven't they got their troubles too
in Andora, Andalusia, Alaska
in the tall tall Andes or
on Alcatraz could I
make my resurrection?

Or would I still wake up, skull
washed by the Western Ocean, nerves
cracked open like the grim Mojave?

What I need is distance,
a word or two with the fat lady
a jig in the rain with the skeleton man
and I'll be ok again, see you

for what they say you are — a man with his hand
firm on the steering wheel
of my father's blue Ford pickup,
sailing through Oregon sunsets, ash lakes

someone driving me home, just driving me home
to Andora, Andalusia, Alaska
that hut in the Andes,
music drifting in across the bay
from the Island of Alcatraz.

I LISTEN TO MARY CROW DOG

I listen to Mary Crow Dog
            It's hard being an Indian woman

I listen to John Trudell
            Duck Valley my Wounded Knee

I listen to Leonard Peltier
            I never killed them agents

I listen to Leonard Crow Dog
            Get rid of the barbed wire mind

            Uncles punch rivets in Belfast.
            Doesn't Belfast box clever,
            just like Jerusalem, Sarajevo
            Fargo, North Dakota?

I hear a voice making stories
of clear runs from Albuquerque

to Deadhorse, Alaska
no borders, no state lines

as the train hurtling north to Canada
falls over itself, swallows its own tail

            dead halt and the raven who is also
            an old woman goes on talking

            Aunts sleep bad in Belfast.
            Doesn't Belfast make the bones ache,
            just like Jerusalem, Sarajevo
            Fargo, North Dakota?

Pedro born under midday firefights
     and the whole prairie burning

Tina and the kids, running through flames
     and the whole prairie burning

Cold Wichita AR15, sere mirage aimed in the wrong direction
     and the whole prairie burning

Crow Dog's prayers razing Terre Haute
     and the whole prairie burning

    goes on talking then stops
    in the split second before
    that forward roll
    starts all the pieces
    falling faultlessly together
    again

        Stepchildren swing on a lazy branch.
           Doesn't Belfast make ghost-
                 dancers of us all?

"I keep having
these visions"
says Coyote
metamorphosing
into a woman —
third time in as many days.

"I don't even
try for them,
run or fast
or pray
for them,
they just happen,
and there's this
voice speaking
from the heel of a green
green island."

Tower cut in glass
road laid in bone
A man, a woman, a child
the bitter taste of stone

"That doesn't sound
like you"
says Beaver.
"Try getting away
for a while,
somewhere new, somewhere
you've never been.
Try starting over again
on your own, from scratch.

You know, maybe
go south."

So Coyote sets out for Vilcabamba,
nice easy pace
no rush
but before she makes
Mesa Verde
the pictures are back
larger than life
projected
on the canyon walls —

no red earth, no blue sky
just white
for miles and miles
just white
biting that weird
fluorescent glitter
of plutonium, uranium, gold.

"This isn't my vision"
says Coyote.
"Belongs to someone else,
someone I haven't dreamed
yet but who's talking
anyways.

Tower cut in glass
road laid in bone
A man, a woman, a child
the bitter taste of stone

That's this someone else's
version of my vision
of the elsewhere I'd
send him back to
if he wasn't already
at home
in his own Rift Valley
on his own Atlantic Rim.

Or maybe that's that
someone else's
slide show
of what the world will look like
when he puts me in
to clutter up
the *mise en scène*."

Coyote hunkers
real troubled
looks down, sees
the Panama Canal,
over her shoulder
there's the forty-ninth parallel,
in the distance
James Bay II.

"Don't worry" says Hare.
"Things'll be ok" says Crow.

Coyote's
not so sure,
she sits tight
on the centre of Turtle's back

thinks about human beings
thinks hard about
a river of them
spilling down from the north
another one
rising up from the south
the people
making themselves at home
on the prairie.

"Here's my vision:
red earth, blue sky
no white
for miles and miles."

Four days later
Coyote stands up
cuts circles around herself
thinks about making
a happy ending
but there's this
interference
this commotion
on the horizon

chanterelles of smoke
exploding
someone shouting
at everybody
else

a dust storm of
blankets
beads
guns
knives.

Even a sly eye
like that
can't walk away
easy
from this one.

Tower cut in glass
road laid in bone
A man, a woman, a child
the bitter taste of stone

A BLUE TATTOO

A blue tattoo
in the shape of the last
wolf seen in these parts:
her left shoulder.

A black and a red tattoo
Imperial dragon rampant
devouring birds of paradise:
his right.

They were conversing about
convergences,
his boat trip up the Meekong Delta, 1967
her last stand at Wounded Knee, 1973

how Spokane Seattle Eugene Vancouver
and Spokane again
inscribed a kind of medicine wheel
where nothing came right.

No one said anything when
the light turned green
and she walked off
against the flow of traffic.

No one noticed when the needle
bled milk and he fell into slow motion,
coal colliding with steel.

No one mentioned the war going on
in the gutter in the blood bank
in the jungle under the tracks

where love lies bleeding in her
lover's sweet home on the range:

a blue and a black
and a red
tattoo.

SÃO PAULO

Once was
a woman living in empty rooms,
a man thinking of a gun, missing.

Elsewhere there was music,
a song about ships and dogs.

There is never enough blue
to fill up the rooms, never enough money
to buy back the gun.

Only the music, rifling the bordellos
scouring the kitchen houses,
razor-backed music
listening for other things:

the Inca Atahualpa
garrotted, weeping gold,
confusion of galleons
breaking up on the coast,
the sound of ricochet
falling out of thunder.

In blue houses money might
fill the distance a field stakes out
between two rivers, a continent
between oceans

but here is
a woman living in empty rooms, a man
thinking of a gun, missing.

SUNLIGHT FROM THIN AIR
after Henry Rollins

out there on the edge, beyond
the great barrier reefs
and the capes of good hope
miracles are being performed:
men walk on water and
women sawn in half, incinerated
by amateur magicians,
put themselves back
together again, get up
and walk away:
salvations to beggar
belief and afterwards
there's enough faith around
to light up half of Brooklyn
enough desire to put you
right back at the centre
if that's where you want to be

but if you're anything like the rest of us
you know the cyclops and the hydra
and especially that larger-than-life-size
snake devouring its own tail
that one in the margins of the margins
of all the maps you've studied
then abandoned
are predictable, that
even the most convincing
miracle, the one that should
bring you to your knees
— *sunlight*
from thin air —

isn't everything, can't
dowse the firestorms or
cut back the tidal waves
blowing out there on the edge
if that's where you want to be

PRINCE FREDRICK'S FEET ARE FLOWERS
after Tom Hart

and everywhere he dances
magnolia, lilac, cherry blossom

that's the fairy tale — on the flip side
Prince Fredrick's feet are shoes

imitation phlox, canvas and polyurethane
$3.99 a pair, made in Taiwan

so when Simple Simon conjures wings
and leaves it all behind

I want to go with him, panniers
of broken dreams strapped to my flanks

but there's Prince Fredrick dancing anyway
bare feet, hot coals

fireweed binding the spine-trellis
consuming the aching cage of ribs

Mr Bojangles, he's dancing for real this time
coppers on his eyes, a bullet between his teeth

fighting fit and just the right kind of hero
for the cold cold days we all fall into

those nights when
Prince Fredrick's feet are flowers

YOU ARE NOT JAMES

In this dream
you are not James.
James is too
busy ordering drinks
(vodka with a straw)
slicing the gold-
breasted steward
with his scimitar stare
to notice the way
you notice
every move he makes.
The others (three
itinerants with blue
dufflebags and windbands
noticing nothing but
the iced-up wings, how
the airplane arches into Oregon)
are not you
either.

There is no double goer
no alter ego
in sight
no one but your lean self
driving into the snow
searching for
the traveller poet's
abominable woman
who appears
then disappears
not once in every
ten years

but once in a lifetime
if you're lucky
and you were lucky
once, at least
that is what you tell me
across a formica table
in a diner in Seattle
where it is bone
cold and no one takes
off hat or coat
hears the turbines howl
or in the middle distance
ravens.

In this dream
you are not James.
James is elsewhere
(Genoa, Algeria, Singapore —
listening to buildings collapse
Einstürzende
the music of the spheres
brought down to base
elements)
while you are here
dealing cards
double-handed
solitaire
at an empty table
that may or may not

be familiar
that double-cross
design feedback
of jet-stream or
someone else's
dream.

OREGON

I sleep with your hair
across my face.
I breathe it in
like water.
In my dreams you die
shot down by sniper fire.
Underground
I eat your bones.

When that
Nootka gave me
salmon for medicine
the fish had your name
on it.

Four years later
it is still swimming
upriver, carrying
everything I know
to be the way things are
and are not
in its silver belly.

STOPPING WITH HORSES

Inside this green rain
he is running to the edge
of a red continent,
its ley lines pathways
cutting deeper than synonyms,
deeper than dreamtime.

He is running to that edge
when six horses stung by headlights
catch him out,
their stippled hides a mapwork
his hands read with the intelligence
of the first cartographer.

The globe tilts on its quivering axis.
It is August on Wolf Hill.
The breathing of horses is its own continent.

NOT SAINT NICK BUT ANANSI

Not Saint Nick but Anansi
you give up what it is
to be sheltering under stone,
hands decked with turquoise
and gold you go
shuffling over the sun
and back again, our
Marco Polo, *voyageur*
with cinnamon, almond
and baskets of orange
moon-fish
you wake us from dreams of drought
to the taste of only water.

THE BEST KIND OF STORY

> *no hands, only silence here*
>
> — Mark Lanegan, *House a Home*

i.

Under blue October moons
you are wearing a cap
tattooed with *Omaha, Nebraska*

a cast-off, you remind me
of my stillborn brother, could as easily
have been driving

that Acadian uncle's
clapped out Thunderbird, west
into the middle distance.

When this conversation begins
there is no dialogue, no
digression, just that snapshot

of your hands
closing on air.
Like fists. A fastness.

ii.

Second time around
the moon's in Leo and we've
both been gone so long

I can't remember your name
and you have forgotten
how to say mine

so I invent one (single
syllable the name of a dog)
and from the first half-sentence

the first improvised line-fall
we both know that this
is going to be the best kind of story

the kind where nothing happens, where
for thirteen months
— beginning, middle, end —

even your Rhodesian ridgebacks
lie down and listen. Episodes unspool,
we travel the desert of songlines

> *Ash Lake, Alcatraz, the disappeared*
> *Jeffrey, John Wayne, Henry Lee*
>
> *Hoover, Nixon, Reagan, Disney*
> *Sub Pop, Peltier, John Trudell*
>
> *juju & voodoo, Rhythm, Skull*
> *okeepa, Bolivia, James & Marcel*
>
> *Ultraman, Spectreman, My Favorite*
> *Martian, Lydia, Henry, Nick*
>
> *jelly beans & jelly babies, Tenochtitlan*
> *"Taillights", "The Ship Song", "Everything"*

iii.

Mornings crash land,
we hear new stars
fall in the ways.

I want to keep on talking (more
tangents, another installment)
but you decide on an ending

that might be a beginning
(salmon feeding frog, killer
whale with the moon in his mouth)

but isn't. *There is no next time
until this time is over.* You said that
once, in your sleep or was it driving

through the seventh month, a cracked November
afternoon on the cusp of the new year
in Oregon, Makah territory, the opening

line of a different story where
actions speak louder than words.
At the end of the day

don't all the tall tales go
back where they belong: underground, rogues
in the element of sinners?

The Angel of Death,
Put in charge of you,
Will duly take your souls:
Then shall ye be brought
Back to your Lord.
                    — *The Koran*, As-Sajda (Sura 32, verse 11)

That warm wind from the west
blew all our houses down

Was it the backwash of wings
or the chinook, arriving early?

In the middle of the room
only a pine table left standing

its smooth planks stained
with ink, the scrimshaw of longing.

No loving-cup, no linen
Azrael sat down opposite

I could see him, so could you
his hands in mine, that are also yours

his gaze the price for calling up
the aerodynamics of departure.

Only Azrael's table left standing
its breadth shouldering famished skies

as the houses are built back up
and the sheep graze their death's-head slopes.

PAPER, GOLD

> *A million candles burnt in him without his being at the trouble to*
> *light a single one.*
>
> — Virginia Woolf, *Orlando*

i.

On just these anniversaries
(May wrestling with thunder,
July got up in hazardous moons)
the women choose to stay indoors,
wandering the safe
constellation of kitchens
or, supine, casting stones and dice
under the netting of a sister's
tropical verandah,
their knowledge of rain cancels out
drum-flare, the felling of pines.

In fields their men build fires.
Every tattoo becomes a fetish,
dim substitute for jasper eyes, those
unringed fingers and cinnabar feet.

I will not say again
what odd cadence fetched me
in from bluffs and the river's back,
how I was listening
to the sound of the words
and not the words themselves
(their unaccounted meanings)
when his laugh called me indigene,
found a different purpose for flesh.

ii.

Thinking to know him
differently (like snow
knows the fretwork
of branches or chrome,
such intimate connections)
I said, *Tell me the meaning*
of your name, its single syllable
a machete in mangrove,
its colour an abrasive
vermillion salute.
Silence is a white bed
stretched taut against
linen possibilities.
It stays that way and dies
cautiously into itself.

iii.

The sea weeps over his wardrobe
of disguises. While I have acquired
the gait of salvaged sailors
on just these anniversaries
— paper, gold —
it is the hands I mourn,
his candles, their creations,
captive in their rehearsed flight.

> *As this occurred to me I lifted my head and a breeze came like*
> *the wind left by the banging front door as Lyle ran away, far*
> *away from me. I knew that whoever he was with I was with too,*
> *and the caresses he was giving to women that I didn't know were*
> *carried across space and time by the hand of God*
> — David Treuer, *Little*

What women know is
some warriors make it back,
their faces like lightning
high up in Jack pine,
that others keep on running,
the lightning alive inside
and burning.

If I go out to wait for him
in that familiar space
between houses and the sea,
watch for his arrival
in the slim blue boat
that was our tree house, our
hideout on winter afternoons
where he balanced below deck
while I sashayed above,
getting my sea legs, learning
to trim the sails
I will not find him
(that look of jasper)
features lit up
like cold water driven
inward and down.

His sudden change of skins
was certain as spring,
the superabundance
of runoff or breakneck tides.
Ravaging line and profile he
pulled down all the shadows
and left me
unsettled as widows are
by thunder, ice storms, granite.

In this photograph
sent from somewhere
in the east
he has cut his hair
and joined the Emperor's
devotion of swordsmen.
He wears the insignia of war,
a trellis of adders
on his left arm
and I am nowhere
to be seen. Outside the frame
carried on breezeway surf
of lilac, my fingers already
trace a different wrist —
one who stayed
dutifully at home,
his body's form

falling, like houses out of a sea,
from my lengthening spine.

What women know is
some warriors make it back,
their faces like lightning
high up in Jack pine,
that others keep on running,
the lightning alive inside
and burning.

DEAD ELEGANT

The pipe
and the woman smoking it

(even
though it belongs
to a man she's
only just met, a foreigner
who signs approval
in blinks and nods
and she's a non-
smoker by nature

but had to know
its smoothness
cradling in her
own exotic hands

like she wanted
to inherit a grand-
father's banjo
and not the violin,
or turn twenty-one
at the Cajun-Creole
heart of south
Louisiana
a sweeter, slower
motion than it's been
back here at home)

her head
bent to the action
of flame and fragrance

is a study in binary
opposition, the chiaroscuro
mirage that stalked
Georges de la Tour
dreaming of *Christ*
in the Carpenter Shop.

"Dead elegant," she says. Meaning
the pipe
and the man smoking it.

ALL SOULS EVE, 1991

When I come to your small house in Ballinteer
harbouring under the soft-spoken Dublin mountains
(third to last in a whitewashed terrace
number 59 Hillview Estate)
your small house purchased with earnings from
the big-time Irish Lotto
I come for nothing in particular, by choice prefer
arriving unannounced, risking deadbolt with vacant drive
or bearing only my diffident sobriquet
a black or white or sometimes blue
feather for entertainment.

When I clatter your letterbox
firing an ecstasy of dog calls
from here to Jack Fox's foothills hideout
I'm not expecting anything
                              but you turn
to making supper anyways.
Your two children (amulets, leaves)
hang from my martyred fingertips.
Spades and brushes
fill my empty hands
and later you feed me
brown beans and white pan
as the sun goes defiantly down.

For the thirty-first time in as many days
I'm caught out by you adopting me
— sister, mother, daughter, sailor —
in the voice of poems

anticipating their own saying, healing me
adroit and unashamed
while your gentle husband, who is also your lover
serves us tea, ouijiing around the kitchen table.
Your deal black kitchen table, a skiff at buoyant harbour
in your small house in Ballinteer.

THE WOMAN AT THE TOP OF THE STAIRS

The woman at the top of the stairs
is my mother.
She is gazing down
the twenty-three treaded steps
and around the bend
into the darkness where I hunker down
under a parlour table
set with roses and calla lilies.
She does not speak but I can hear her
calling my name, a fractured
falling cry that brushes the biting reds
and the starched collars
of the lilies.
The year is 1847
and today is my father's funeral.
(I saw him kill mice, rabbits, a fox
and once, in the dead of winter, a wolf
lean and already half gone.
He was not a hunter or a tracker but
as my mother used say, "Simply a bold man,
and a brute.")
I hold a spider, daddy-long-legs,
captive in a musty clay pickle jar.
Under the cork I feel her
conserving energy, refusing to breathe,
to spin or build or hunt.
When the woman at the top of the stairs
tilts that predictable
fraction of an inch forward
I will unstop the jar
watch her skittle sideways into dark
as the woman's hand opens and closes
on emptying air.

BONE MAKING, THE BEAVER

i.

On the bank of the Beaver River
there is a tree with thirteen candles
awake in its branches,

heavy limbs cradling
the wrapped bodies
of our several grandmothers.

This is their valley
and they live in it now
as they have always lived in it

at midwinter, filling up with snow
at midsummer, an iron sun scouring
ridges scythed in glacier thrash.

It is mid-October and I am
searching for her shape
— Rebecca Amelia Parslow Hardy, Scots-Irish woman,
Pelajia Lara Two Wolves, Ojibwa-Cree woman —
her apple breath, her flint teeth, musk scent of leaves
mouldering under limestone.

Her bones are the black branches
of trees opening against hunter moons,
grandmother who talks to us in dreams.

ii.

When our mother was nine
a ghost walked down the attic stairs.
He was wearing the buffalo robe
and carrying her mother's harpsichord

as if it were the eucharist
or some other sacred object.

She recognized him for a longhair,
one of the old ones who wouldn't leave,
who'd die before he'd change his ways.

She left out pans of water, warmed-over maple syrup
berries, bark — food he wouldn't touch.

Because she was an only child it was easy
to slip back up the attic stairs,
see distances from the crow's nest.

"When I draw a picture," she said
"it is not myself but someone
you think I look like."

When she was thirteen the longhair came back,
walked out of the woodlot, across the lawn
turned into the road without glancing back.

iii.

Somewhere in the middle distance
the camera lost its slender focus and I
fell into her two hands in a yellow room
at the foot of the valley.

1960. The world started running
in the opposite direction.

iv.

April and the windows are high,
open to the east. There is snow on the sill.

The turquoise air is leafing
Manitoba maple, forget-me-nots.

I favour the spring because our mother does.
Because she pulls the sheets tight
as prairie ice, paints her own
room white enamel, papers it
with stars, chevrons, clover.

Because her hands like her words
are sure of themselves,
never fall down.

When I was nine
my brother was seven.
The third child
lost in a summer thunderstorm
spoke to us: "Christmas," he said.
"I should have been born
at Christmas."

She slept for four days while we
dreamed she would never wake up.
In October she went back to work and I
sat on the white fence
swaying, saying nothing.

Our grandfather talked about the boy,
"He was a longhair, the one that got away,
slipped back into the shadows, a fish."

v.

She remembers her mother at the piano
or out gathering eggs before six.

Tatting. Mending.
Making maple sugar.

The house was big, a farmhouse
echoing with *Rock of Ages*
and in December *I Saw Three Ships*.

She remembers her mother
doing everything
that had to be done.

vi.

You live away. At the dead centre
of a continent that dreamed itself
into existence, cornucopiaed
in corn, pear, apple, gooseberry,
currant, blackberry, blueberry, squash.
All the intricate vines.

You live at home.
The rift valleys in your wrists
the jagged bluffs, the drumlins
dreaming in your joints and hollows,
were landscapes I gave names to
then departed.

Today distance sits like a stone
swallowed by a fierce bird
impossible to dislodge.

Which month will I find you
in a tree on the bank of the Beaver?

Will we talk then,
Rebecca, Pelajia, you and I?

Part Two

But you I have no distance from. Every move you make feels like I'm traveling in your skin; every glance you take out the window, as though you were completely alone and dreaming in some other time. It does no good to wave my arms. Now everything's reversed.

— Sam Shepard, *Cruising Paradise*

A TREE ASLEEP AT THE CENTRE OF A FIELD

A tree asleep at the centre of a field
dreams of peripheries — a new post
on the river's collarbone with no
visible means of support.

Like my dream of saying "I love you"
in another language, one that has invented
vocabularies for gesture, silence, the long-drawn
dissonance of breathing on your own.

What part of me has travelled the fabular distance
to arrive at cities impossible as this one
will collude like any man
                    in devising right relations,
the actual dimensions
                    of influence and difference.

What part of me has never left
our fathers' or our mothers' hill-grey dwellings
(his afternoons of thunder, her evenings framed in fire)
makes covenant for you in far-off places

Tsitika, where the morning does all the talking,
Tagish, where the measured conversations
that drive women and their men to the broken-hearted heights
of Golan or Estelí are beyond even the dreams of trees.

A GEOGRAPHY OF SOULS

Your handwriting reversed
in the concave mirror
(its shy surfaces
garlanded with winter)
discloses a fluid calligraphy —

　　　　millrace, aqueduct, the tidal draw
　　　　of underwater caves
　　　　where swimmers go to drown,
　　　　their bodies inscribing
　　　　the lightest stroke of all.

What goes unnoticed
in the writing on the wall,
in every disquisition
on the species of love
or the nature of missives,

　　　　makes up a geography
　　　　of souls, a code
　　　　all colour and deepline:
　　　　a swift swimming the windowpane or
　　　　your handwriting, reversed.

IF THE SEA BECOMES ORDINARY

As difficult a journey as any
voyage between continents locked
in their vacancy of air miles, this
trying not to think of you

is like bringing that ghost horse
home from the sea, his raised
head scenting rain from the west

or coaxing a tantrum-child
from sun-struck eel-grass,
taste of earth delighting blood.

If the sea becomes ordinary
I will lose you as the hunchback comet
elides into hails of light

the sea which in any weather
is always more than itself,
is an amulet cut from jasper
or the skull of an Inca dreamer
trying not to think
of the consequences of rain
or the drift of absence.

A FLICK OF THE WRIST

Cities, counties, hamlets, crossroads are
figments in the mind's acquisitive eye
when you speak their long-shot names:

Phoenix to Amarillo, our twinned figures
dissolve in a February heat wave.
Calais to Esterhausen, where we count on
crucial frosts to mask a brevity of reds and greens,
the regalia of border crossings.

You want to see things in a different light
while I desire primary landscapes:
turquoise, cochineal, malachite

something earthed yet dissident,
the planetarium and the bibliothèque
inverted but seeding our garden
with new stars and ingenious stories.

What's needed is neither distance
nor an approximate edge.
Just the usual flick of a wrist,
deft observation of that homely
west-by-northwest inclining angle
we both failed to take into account.

If ever I wed you, I wed you
there and then.

On the height of Paris
with autumn and the barbarous
European winter closing in
we stood together
under the four-poster, canopied
bed of the central nave.

And while Father Gatineau transfigured
into the twelfth disciple (Saint John
reminding us *Car Dieu a tant aimé le monde*
qu'il a donné son Fils unique . . .)
you touched my hand so lightly
leaving was a mark
entirely outside the question.

I'd been contemplating the distance
between the four imagined corners of the earth,
between Rilke and Rimbaud
and especially Emily Dickinson
(that incandescent *heft*
of cathedral tunes).

I'd been noting the likeness of those four granite
featherweight angels of the Apocalypse
posted sky-high in shadow and frankincense
to your profile at all the portals,
all the doors and windows, corbels and cornerstones
of my waxen days and juniper nights.

I'd been weighing chance and coincidence
against salvation and love as acts of the will

when this red, gold and white acolyte
raised his right hand and blessed us —
In nomine Patri, et Fili
et Spiritus Sancti. Amen.

A voice that loves then leaves us
vagrant in cities continued like this one,
where consolation is a dream
and guardian angels a figment
of every beggar's imagination but my own
whose turn it is now to take
two steps forward, turn over
under the counterpane and find
in living wingspans your words
defining a sacred blue heartland:

If ever I wed you, I wed you
here and now.

VENEZIA

Here is the photo
that was never taken
that day in April
in Venice.

It is somewhere near
the Bridge of Sighs,
there are others just like it
all trying to catch
those whispers
the perfect backdrop to
a kiss.

Look, you cannot see the bridge
or the canal
or the gondolier
who should have been there
either.

Instead there is someone
striding out of the frame
(you can see the shadow)
going who knows what
distance to unmask himself
for the woman
in *appartamento* 1859.

All petals and glass
she's the dream he's having
but it doesn't matter
(they're hanging two Frenchmen
in the square, preparing to
take the tongues of their
Austrian cohorts)

he loves her
you can hear him
say it.

In this picture
boats are leaving.
The Lido is a fire of rapiers,
the Doge's palace consumed.

FLOOR MOSAICS, SAINTE-CHAPELLE

Caught out
in a clover leaf of stars
we are
twinned
identical
two wolves
nosing around the golden egg
scenting eternal splendour
turning tail on that something
it's easier to ignore:

the vigilant goose
hovering overhead, sepia
Loki-bird who'll always
make it there first.

Even Courtaud and the desperate
packs come down on ice-locked Paris
couldn't have what's already
laid in stone:
the intricate eventuality
of a mosaicized wilderness.

A harpsichord does not build itself:
A family is a harpsichord.

— Paul Durcan, *Sunday's Well*

i.

The moon is full with December.
All day we have traced it
a wafer gaining weight, growing
ready for breaking.

One star, the planet Venus,
pegs the sun-split afternoon
to indigo evening, the indelible
going down of months of reckoning.

Under it Belfast idles, brittle between festivals,
births, the old year and the new.
This is your hour. Janus-faced it hangs
a bridge suspended, ready before you are.

Your father reading Hughes and Gellner
(*the breakdown of cultures*)
his bare arms the arms of a boy
about to enter the sea, is all oriental composure.

All hectic optimism I am
well back on the shore, still building
like the architect unwilling to quit
his halcyon galleries, their original shining cupolas.

ii.

At the going down of sun
came three beasts:
Lupa/ Equa/ Strix
Wolf/ Horse/ Owl.

Midwives, totems, shepherds and kings
out of a wilderness of affirmations
they entered my bloodstream,
there to see you through.

iii.

Wolf told of running to ground
making shelter in a clean space
smelling of earth and pine.
She taught me not to speak,
how to conserve everything.

Gave me eye teeth, a posture,
a way in to the cave at the centre,
got me down on all fours
panting and listening for every
aqueous, suboptical
pitch our straining bones
our plaited fibres together
were bound to reach.

When she left it was
shell fire
meteor light
weird pibrochs
night.

iv.

Out of the painted desert
the fifth horse of the Apocalypse
— riderless, unbroken, burning —
all Aztec eye, Paiute nostril
saying: *Annunciation, annunciation,*
              Resurrection, resurrection

She taught me to breathe
deep, fast, strong — and hold.
Throat stripped and still releasing
the screams of mares, hides flaming.
This is called oxygenating the universe.
This is called breathing for two.

v.

Owl was sheer beak and claw
sickle, scythe, scimitar
taking aim and hitting home
gold eye an amulet. I am bewitched
and have the voice of creatures
stripped from the sky and falling
wingless to earth.

vi.

After the animals: pain, and the memory of pain
                    receding
                    water, and the sluice of water
                    diluted
                    hands, and the force of hands
                    abating

elide with a sudden weightlessness
(I am thin as a wafer, broken)
and the unexpected sheen
(milk scents, rose tints)
of you our child, sky daughter
riven, hale, arrived
from deep space, the vaults
of story, the squared regions
of our free thinking.

Behind, beside, around it all
the voice, the hands, the halo
of this man who
      — singular as a guard in a gatebox
         lone as the angel in the garden —
husbands me
with towels and sponges
with tea and toast
with the small mouth drinking me,
who tells of meteor showers in the east
and the city briefly at ease with itself.

"A family is a constellation.
One, two, three . . . Look.

There is strength in numbers."

SHORELANDS

I will live with you
in a house made of lavender
and pine, a house that is a ship
heading east by south east
a longboat painted
with the eyes of dragons
fortified
with the armour of angels.

I will make you
a wedding song
of paper and crayons
and the child
will watch out for the moon,
her window
Elaine's tower.

There is sailing
and there is sailing.
This is not a ship
going nowhere, it is
the great blue heron
awkward and ignited
by its own certainty
in the course of things.
Flying without instruments

we arrive, touch down, depart.

I WALK WITH MY FINGERS IN THE AIR

Air is a leopard, a lynx, an ocelot,
a sun-scored, tessellated body
through whose windows I cast
lifelines, tow ropes out to listening leaves.

A snail's horn my index
finger deciphers alder root
and oak bole, the traces
sea slug and hermit crab
compose between boisterous tides.

I walk with my fingers in the air,
a Kirov ballerina or a Hotspur kicker
sending messages — a string
of *e*'s and *u*'s — confirmation of my own blue voice
ripping in savage wind.

Between glide and falter
I grow into myself, falling
dans ma peau. Rugged
as any sunset cowboy I sidle
towards my solstice birthday,
risky fingers in the air.

LUPO

There is a single
blue room in the house.
In it a child asleep
hands like starfish
feet like bruised paws
in snow. She sleeps
without seeming to breathe.

Your child
or mine?
Already she is
climbing trees
eating air
demolishing stars
counting fish.
Already she is lying
back to back
with the blue-grey
wolf-dog who's taken
winter residence
in our woodshed.
Was it this afternoon
she ran circles
around that spooked
pine marten?

"I will speak to you,"
she says
"without making
a sound,
I will tell you
about the animals

that come with the moon
and go with the sun,
arrive dreaming
torn, fragrant
leave wide
awake and hungry
as knives."

Her voice is
geyser and backwash,
her language
could be Welsh
or Mandan,
the long distance
courtship of wolves.

Neither yours
nor mine,
belonging already
out there among them.

A BLUE DRESS
for Medbh McGuckian

Without the awkwardness of invitations
you arrive in the snow
of pale days unraveling another year
we hold back from naming

to give my daughter a blue dress, all bustle and crinoline,
that was your daughter's zone for make believe.
It is her fifth birthday and you are still
teaching me how to be her mother.

The ravening heights, the coy, capricious turns
it takes to call up the creatures of Emily and Jane,
the solo *pas de deux* chipped out
of speechless Sunday afternoon retreats

are ghostings of your Emer's elegant
manoeuvres (her translucent shutters shut on
weeping birch combing sheets of winter rain)
and at the heart of every straying execution

the glass box that is a promise
of spring visits, summer conversations.
Later you will tell me your poems are children
precocious, grass-fed, fall-over-themselves heavy

with expectation. And I will tell you mine are bones cast out
from the overburdened body of the moon. We will talk
about ocean-going men we both have known
and the difficulty of finding a comfortable chair in any house.

But right now there are candles, and the business
of lighting them, blowing out, lighting again.

SAULT STE. MARIE

i.

You were driving that
'79 Chrysler Cordoba
just for the exotic
sound of the name,
I was shored up
in Toronto, you
hadn't arrived but were
heading north
from West Texas, you couldn't
master the dialect
or the politic
turn of phrase
and how much further
could anything be
than the Sault?

If you'd arrived on time
the whole story might have
turned out differently.
There were faults on both sides:
the mechanic's son who
liked to let things ride,
your lack of sleep and failure
to make head or tail
of maps and that crow
dead in the middle of the road.

And I couldn't hear you coming
all those nights through Minnesota sleet,
struggling up the underwater cable
in someone else's movie.

If you'd made it
any day in 1985
I would have recognized your
silhouette —
a figure knee deep in snow
shouldering a satchel
of basalt chippings, four
blue felt pens and the photo
of a nameless brother.

ii.

Tonight there are candles
in a white drift, it could be
Rancho Bernardo
where your father died
or Artemesia Street
where mine was born.

There is nothing but air
between and there are
forty-four flames
one for every falling
fallen year.
Your daughter's hands
are the span of a maple leaf,
mine are the span of two.
We give you a red French
Canadian toque
so you won't get lost in the snow
again.

i.

Driving north
we sight a ziggurat
of sorts.
What new religion
has sprung up
among the pines?
The plains of south-
western Ontario run
to distances our land-
locked tarns find
difficult to imagine.

ii.

For Sky, a tree house.
Covenanted in maple,
lilac, the onset of gooseberry
it is grotto, tabernacle, ark.
Limitless preserve
from whose mineshaft
we hear her voice calling
on the local *lares* and *penates*.

iii.

In Benares
a Shaolin blow-in
listens to loons touch down
on the stooped shoulder
of Lake Superior.

He writes to her,
his long lost daughter,
not in English
but in Cree,
turns to find the temple door
blazingly ajar.

RANCHO BERNARDO
in memoriam Henry Carson Aughey

Midnight and two
hours later, no warning
just that dream
about an airplane then
a minor tremor
at the edge of the earth:
your father asleep in San Diego
his heart unexpectedly stopped.

"This is the last story
the final lesson
I have for you:
It was as easy as
putting in the afternoon
shooting baskets,
every one a winner,
as easy as keeping off
those storm clouds
and the rain I knew would never
touch my skin."

When I answer the phone
you have already covered your eyes
with your hands.
It is Christmas in Drumbeg
Hilden, Belfast,

frost but no snow and everywhere you look
a bed of bones.

So many things you never
told your father
before he died;
so many I am learning
how to say to mine.

YOUR CALL
in memoriam Jean Isabel McCracken

I am calling you
from outer space, from heaven
or the other side
of the Philippine Trench.

Still the black sheep
I always was,
I'm ringing up
to tell you

our secret life
(clandestine trysts
in smoking zones,
Zen and zabaglione
on the sly)

survives.

My mouth to your ear
tells a short story
that goes on and on.

Whatever I say you will see
that October photograph,
the one your father took
near Massey:

myself decked out in hunting gear,
Billy beside me straddling
the exodus of a first bike,
the river falling down behind us.

There is the maw of silence
and I know you're at a loss
for words. Still, it's your call.

Whatever I say
we are both here
listening.

THE WOLF DISAPPEARS
in memoriam Wesley Lawrence McCracken

I rev the engine seven times.
The seventh son of the seventh son
of a seventh son — the luckiest
of all the lucky ones —
Septimus, I call myself,
Septimus
getting ready for the last flight,
the Mosquito heading out
from Halifax.

I do not have the heart
of a warrior.
I do not have the stomach
or the bowels
for war.
Long-sighted and sporting
the hands of a Class A mechanic
I will build or rebuild
any motor between Goose Bay
and Esquimalt
but I will not fight.

My idea of freedom
is a black Labrador
let off the leash
in a field of February snow
or the wolf when it
disappears under the treeline,
spiky frame jack-
rabbiting tamarack runways.

No grease monkey I,
a high-flyer through and through.
Fifty-five years spent
serving God and country
after my own fashion:
pumping gas and changing tires
keeping the boys on and off the road
deciphering the winedark enigma
of valves and hoses, ratchets and jacks.

Despite the blackest November
in Canadian history
I am revving the Mosquito's engine
louder than I have ever revved it before
just for the crystalline pitch, the whine —
defying the winter to ice my wings
or bring the pair of us down
one single revolution
before we're ready
to go.

GREEN POOL WITH LIGHTNING

in memoriam Shirley Valerie McCracken Marshall

Our faces ring the circumference
of a bluestone well, making their
circle around her —
porthole; iris; sunspot;
the halo of a candle.

She is all our mothers,
we are every one
of her children.
She is not drowning.
She is not waving, either.

This is not a cancer ward.
It is a green pool
and she is swimming, her laugh
the radiant collision
of lightning into water

or a trapline
with every mechanism sprung
wide open, the ghost of a chance
escaping into conifers,
the sidereal lull of Sarawak wood.

Our watching is a wreath
of sweetgrass. It is burning
and we are letting her leave,
a winter mink into the snowscape,
spring salmon arcing back over
bales of air, into water.

CANADIAN SLEEP

in memoriam William Edward McCracken

i. July, 1942

Marie, last night I dreamed
of five sons
and your sleeping body
bedded down
under star blankets.

Yesterday
was my sixteenth birthday,
mother weeping
in the twelfth of July sun,
her hands white
seabirds signalling
farewells to the
Isle de France.

Today
the North Atlantic
is a vault between us
and this European war
obscures the features
of your aching hours.

If there are sons
I know I will leave them
making apologies
for having been
away at all.

ii. December, 1944

Dorsal gunner
on the plains beyond
Hilversum

I'm holed up
in Nijmegen pasture-
land, the jackboots
of the Third Reich
scandalising my Dutch
defenders: Karl de Boer
and his elegant *vrouw*
holding hands
behind their backs.

There is a wych elm
floorboard and less
than one inch
of braided seagrass
between me and the end
of the world.

iii. February, 1945

In Edinburgh, in The North Briton
I drink two pints of heavy
with my brother, Wes.

Wes whose hands I have not seen
in two and a half years:
my mother's hands
churning barrels of butter.

iv. April, 1945

Only God and a Scotch thistle
will ever know
how close I came
to never coming back.

How close we all come
at least once or twice
to that.

It was an act of the will
such as neither my heroic father
nor my brave brothers
nor even my death-defying sisters
could have called up.

The tank blossoming
in a calendula of flame
and my hand, my bare hand
prising the iron turret hatch
open
open
open

v. October, 1945

Friedrich Mues
lived and died
in Hagen.
A raw bird, a scavenger
a soldier
I will give his *soldbuch*

(its missing photo
its torn facts
windfall for my
shocked hands)
to my youngest niece's
husband, a man like myself
who's used to pack drill
and bayonet practice,
for safekeeping.

vi. *January, 1947*

Twenty months
and counting
the miles from scorched
Rhine-bank
to scoured Southampton,
the *Queen Elizabeth*
docked and throbbing
in shafts of unearthly light.

vii. *June, 1984*

Alive in two continents
I spent my life with you.

In showers of sparks
I spent my life with you.

Behind a welder's mask
I spent my life with you.

On the crest of a hill looking over the valley
I spent my life with you.

In a torrent of affection
I spent my life with you.

Marie.

viii. August, 1995

Five sons and at the height
of summer their women
watching our grandchildren
spitting out watermelon pips.

For Jesse
I have made the perfect car,
knitting together five precious metals.

For Dylan
I have cut and hammered
a forest of birdhouses.

For Cody and Tyler
I have posed under
just the right fall of light.

For the girls
all of them, there will be gardens
acres of gardens.

ix. July, 1998

I remember Lee George,
that Ojibwa from Colpoy's
Bay, saying over and over
in the trench-black night:

Death should come fronting
Death should come fronting

A hard thing, then
to gaze down the barrel
of a loaded pistol

to look a Pomeranian grenadier
square in the eye, to camp out together
on prairies of slaughter.

A hard thing, now
to step out of the shadows
with my photographs
and my medal of honour

stop jumping out of my skin
when Lavender's Chevy backfires,
shrapnel flexing under my toes.

Death should come fronting
Death should come fronting

Stilled by a Canadian sleep
no koans, no qualms, no delays:
it's all air now

all air, Marie, and pine cones.

THEATRE FIVE
for Dr HR McClelland

The hands have it,
they perform miracles.
So, though, do the eyes.
They confer faith
hope, charity: these three.

Driving the lough shore
into Belfast City Hospital in the rain
I am watching my son play rugby
in Zimbabwe, his golden arms
lifting the ball
out of the golden air

and I am thinking how it is
to be a forty-three-year-old woman
in Ward 4 South — Cancer Treatment Centre —
terminal and determined to hang-glide
out over the Azores, henna-brunette hairpiece
displayed like wings.

My son is a virtuoso, the acme
of good judgement. It's that flair
for precision and fine-line
I catch hold of, run with
every time I set the scalpel
— immaculate, neat — against skin.

Like love, surgery is an act of the will.
It is my art and I do it well:
sheer courage, sheer conviction, the blunt end of necessity.
Some of the women will get up and
others of them will not. I know this
and I honour them all

from a distance. And when I drive
back home out of Belfast in the rain
the flame of a smile drifting up
out of ether — that vital sign —
is what keeps me going:
clean line bisecting the deepest horizon.

The hands have it.
So, though, do the eyes.
They confer faith
hope, charity: these three.

ACER RUBRUM

At home in Flesherton
five dead, five of seven
brothers and sisters
and I am a red maple,
sentinel at the corners
of Peter Street
and Elizabeth Lane,
year in, year out
standing hard against gales
willfully robust,
singularly serene.

I dream of blood-
lines and oncogenes but
the sap shoots, liquid amber
jetting up and down my spine.
My fingertips drip
syrup, I am out in the wind
and will not come in.

My daughter has not died.
She is bedding the roots
of larch and rowan.
When I look in at her
window she is making ready
for another Christmas,
her hands cupping
a fragrant flame,
her whole body a screen
between my angle of vision
and a corrosive, ink-black sky.

Rushing the bars
cuttle-bone blunt
bump of snout,
panoptic primordial
eye were more than
mechanical,
something that haunted
the cobalt distance,
indifferent observation
a code for promise.

Featherweight exodus

(the cage a dazzling
rictus in outback sun)

blue freefall
into blue.

But the brain was not
quick enough to name
the ripped-out skein of gut
for what it was. Instead
it took that silver taste
of blood to wake him
wake him
wake him up.

Now he just swims.
Holding it all
at a distance.
The landlocked debates
about heredity and environment,
gene-pools and therapies.

Now he just swims
and the shadows
out there circling
beyond those twinned headlands
may or may not carry
the burden of their own weight.

Twenty-five funerals, one
for every year
of a life lived north
and darker
than this invisible
Maginot line
decides it might have been.

One for every year
and two unattended
(*it always rests*
uneasily)
twin bullets lodged
under the breastplate,
a double
bill of open endings.

I am watching you on tv
I am watching you in yet
another dream —
front-rolling out from under
burning aircraft,
escaping from Alcatraz,
falling asleep at the wheel.

But when you fly by night
coming home from the west, from Juneau
Alaska to that gap in the Black Mountains
there will be just enough
space for a fighter pilot
to sight the flare-
path, find clearance,
coast the hemi-plain
out to mazarine seas.

GOOD FRIDAY, BELFAST, 1998

i.

Later in the day
our daughter says
the snow is an angel's wing
folded over Knockagh,
or the tongue of an ox
licking salt.

At 6am I found you
walking in sleep, trying
to make sense of a dream
about a soldier
knee-deep in Brueghel's
Massacre of the Innocents.

My own dream
was smaller:
three gentle men
and a lady
sitting to draughts
in a moated castle.

> *We are all*
> *dreaming the same dream.*

ii.

I am squinting down the shaft
of a splintered telescope, trying to catch
a glimpse of the goings-on
over at Stormont.

Your eyes are wide open,
gaze back at the camera, saying
everything is in motion,
still.

We are waiting for a sign, for the idiom
to cut a new skin. The language wants
to alter so dramatically
it acquires a new vocabulary.

Not an execution, but miracles.
Not fixity, but faith.
Nothing but the bottom line

will satisfy the look of honesty
on the face of that young man
and the woman old enough to be his mother

the pair of them
standing like the rest of us
up to our oxters in snow, in salt.

> *Aren't we all*
> *Dreaming the same dream?*

SAUDADE

The Portuguese "saudade" is frequently translated into English as "homesick." Perhaps the most accurate gloss on this indelible Portuguese word is by Nick Cave who, in his lecture *The Secret Life of the Love Song* (1998), describes it as "an inescapable longing, an unnamed and enigmatic yearning of the soul . . . the desire to be transported from darkness into light, to be touched by the hand of that which is not of this world."

EXILE WOMAN

During the seventeenth century, it was not uncommon for Ireland to be referred to as Wolfland because of the island's high population of wolves. While in England wolves were exterminated by 1509, and in Scotland by 1684, it was 1786 before deforestation, Cromwellian legislation and the work of professional hunters wiped out Irish wolves. Although the last verifiable wolf kill occurred in County Carlow, numerous places throughout the country lay claim to the same achievement. Wolves in the province of Ulster were most likely erased by the 1690s, but local legend in County Antrim has it that the last wolf in Ireland was shot and killed on Wolf Hill, a once wooded prominence now part of the Ligoniel area of North Belfast.

SKUSHNO

The Austrian writer Gregor von Rezzori begins his *Memoirs of an Anti-Semite: A Novel in Five Stories* (1969; 1981) with the following: "*Skushno* is a Russian word that is difficult to translate. It means more than dreary boredom: a spiritual void that sucks you in like a vague but intensely urgent longing."

ETERNITY IS NOW

A parable in Friedrich Nietzsche's *The Gay Science* (1882; 1887) tells of a madman swinging a lantern in the sunlit morning market and crying, "I am looking for God! I am looking for God!" When a group of atheists jeer his behaviour, the madman asks, "Where has God gone? . . . I shall tell you. *We have killed him — you and I.*"

I LISTEN TO MARY CROW DOG

Mary Brave Bird is a Brule Sioux from the Rosebud Reservation in South Dakota. In 1971 she joined the recently formed American Indian Movement and her son, Pedro, was born at Wounded Knee during the siege in 1973. She later married Leonard Crow Dog, a Lakota Sioux leader in the Native American Church and AIM's foremost medicine man. Leonard Crow Dog was convicted on trumped-up charges relating to Wounded Knee and the 1975 incident at Oglala and served two years of a twenty-three-year sentence in a series of penitentiaries including Terre Haute in Indiana. Mary Crow Dog's autobiography, *Lakota Woman* (1990), chronicles her personal struggles and those of the movement during the 1960s and 1970s. Also a member of AIM, Leonard Peltier is an Ojibwa-Sioux from Turtle Mountain, South Dakota. In June 1975 he was involved in a shootout between FBI agents and AIM defenders on the Pine Ridge Reservation in South Dakota, in which two agents and one Native man died. Following the incident, Peltier was indicted on murder charges. Among the evidence suppressed by the prosecution during his trial in Fargo, North Dakota, were FBI lab reports indicating that the Witchita AR-15 rifle believed to be the murder weapon could not have fired the shots which killed the agents. Even so, Peltier was convicted on two counts of murder in the first degree and on 1 June 1977 he was sentenced to two consecutive life terms in federal prisons, which he is still serving. John Trudell is a Santee Sioux who was AIM's national chairman and one of the prime movers behind Peltier's Defense Committee, an organisation dedicated to gaining public support for a new trial. His Paiute-Shoshone wife Tina was a leader in the fight for water rights on the Duck Valley Reservation in Nevada. On the night of 11 February 1979 Tina Trudell, her mother and the three Trudell children died in an arson attack on their Duck Valley home. Among the most notable accounts of these and related lives and events are Peter Matthiessen's *In The Spirit of Crazy Horse* (1983; 1991) and Leonard Peltier's *Prison Writings: My Life is My Sun Dance* (1999).

RED EARTH, BLUE SKY

When in 1535 the Inca Manco, the puppet ruler placed on the throne by the Spaniards, revolted against his masters, he retreated deep into the

Amazon forest where he developed a settlement called Vilcabamba. For over 200 years archaeologists speculated about its location until in the 1980s Espiritu Pampa, a site at the headwaters of the Amazon, was identified as the actual "lost city of the Incas."

The cliff dwellings at Mesa Verde in south-western Colorado were the home of the Anasazi. This nomadic people moved onto the mesa top in the sixth century and became agriculturalists. Their settled culture grew increasingly complex and the elaborate stone villages built into the cliffs of Mesa Verde mark the culmination of 700 years of community living and aesthetic refinement. By 1300, however, the dwellings had been abandoned, most likely due to drought and an increase in hostile raids. Today, twenty-four Native American peoples, including the Hopi and the Pueblo, have an ancestral affiliation with the sites at Mesa Verde.

SÃO PAULO

Atahualpa was the favourite son of Huayna Capac, Inca of Peru. When his father died in 1525, Atahualpa inherited only a portion of the Inca empire; his half-brother and the legitimate heir, Huáscar, assumed the position of Inca. Later, Atahualpa invaded Huáscar's domains, defeated and imprisoned his half-brother, and made himself Inca. On 16 November 1532, Atahualpa met Francisco Pizarro at Cajamarca. Invited into the city, Atahualpa was seized and imprisoned. He offered to fill the room in which he was held once with gold and twice with silver. At the same time, he secretly ordered the death of Huáscar. During the next four months nearly 8 tonnes of gold were accumulated, but in return Pizarro had Athualpa tried for his brother's murder and for plotting against the Spanish. Pizarro then baptised Atahualpa before having him publicly strangled.

PRINCE FREDRICK'S FEET ARE FLOWERS

Prince Fredrick's Feet (1991) is the title of a self-published mini-comic book created by the New York writer and illustrator Tom Hart. It tells the story of a con man named Prince Fredrick and two lookers-on, the not-so-gullible Willie and his sceptical sidekick Simon, at the local Flower Festival.

VENEZIA

Between 23 April and 8 July 1859, the Austrian empire and an alliance of French and Italian forces were at war over Lombardy and the Austrian-occupied territory which now constitutes north-eastern Italy. When an armistice was signed at Villafranca the Austrians had abandoned Lombardy but still held Venice. Consequently, Italian nationalists felt betrayed by their French supporters and in certain quarters began to turn against them.

FLOOR MOSAICS, SAINTE-CHAPELLE

Now surrounded by the Palais de Justice, Sainte-Chapelle on Paris's Ile de la Cité is a palatine gothic chapel built in 1248 by King Louis IX. Its purpose was to house holy relics (believed to be the crown of thorns and part of the cross) purchased at extortionate rates by Louis from the bankrupt empire of Byzantium. While the lower chapel is dark and close, the upper one is a "jewel box" of fifteen stained glass windows depicting scenes from the Old and New Testaments. This abundance of light and colour tends to eclipse the remarkable floor mosaics in the high chapel, which boast a skilful design of paired wolves and open-winged geese.

The anonymous *Journal d'un Bourgeois de Paris*, composed between 1405 and 1449, describes events in Paris during part of the Hundred Years War and mentions a winter so severe that wolves roamed the outskirts of the city. Based on this and other fifteenth-century accounts of a large wolf reputed to have killed fourteen people, Daniel Mannix's novel *The Wolves of Paris* (1978) tells the story of a legendary wolf-dog called Courtaud, the leader of a pack of wolves which besieges the starving city before being destroyed by a cunning *louvetier*.

GOOD FRIDAY, BELFAST, 1998

The Belfast Agreement of 10 April 1998 set a framework for the devolution of power to a new Assembly in Northern Ireland. The objective of the Agreement was to achieve a stable accommodation between Irish Nationalism and Ulster Unionism. An important expectation of the Agreement was that all paramilitary groups would commit themselves to a process of disarmament. At the time of writing, this has yet to be achieved.

AGMV Marquis

MEMBER OF SCABRINI MEDIA

Quebec, Canada
2002